T0210075

A BITTER SWEET MOMENT

ARRONDA MOSLEY

authorHOUSE®

AuthorHouse™
1663 Liberty Drive
Bloomington, IN 47403
www.authorhouse.com
Phone: 1 (800) 839-8640

Scripture taken from The Holy Bible, King James Version. Public Domain

Published by AuthorHouse 06/29/2019

ISBN: 978-1-7283-1747-2 (sc)
ISBN: 978-1-7283-1745-8 (hc)
ISBN: 978-1-7283-1746-5 (e)

Library of Congress Control Number: 2019908706

Print information available on the last page.

This book is printed on acid-free paper.

A Bittersweet Moment

This is a work that touches the heart and soul in a profound way. We are candidly and poignantly introduced to a beautiful family, one that is perfectly imperfect, much like all of ours. We join their journey, and experience their triumph as our deepest fears of potentially fatal illness, accidents, horrific incidents and loss of loved ones are confronted. We learn the true value of time, and love. We see the power of forgiveness, the limitless power of faith and how trust in God proves to be what truly saves us all ultimately. I can tell you as both a breast cancer survivor and one who has suffered the loss of my Mother, that this book is a must read. It will move you in unexpected ways. This intimate story provides comfort and a graceful path to surviving a few of the hardest moments life offers all of us at one point or another.

5 Stars for A Bittersweet Moment!
Kathy Kowalski

CONTENTS

Chapter 1: Family 1

Chapter 2: Round One—The C Word 11

Chapter 3: The Power of Forgiveness! 17

Chapter 4: Round Two—It's Back! 29

Chapter 5: The Preparation 39

Chapter 6: When God Cleans You Up 55

Chapter 7: Last Birthday .65

Chapter 8: Bittersweet Moment 73

Chapter 9: Letting Go 85

I dedicate this book to my children, Tynisha Savage, Tyron Hurst, and Lakeisha Smith. I thank you for your unconditional love and support that helped me complete this project.

CHAPTER 1

~

FAMILY

There isn't a day that goes by that I don't think about my mother, Helen C. Harris, who was affectionately known as Christine (Chrissy). She was born on June 15, 1941. She was the mother of four children. She had two girls and two boys and married to Robert Harris. Mom was the youngest of eight children born to the late Della and Othar Hurst Sr. She had five sisters and two brothers.

My mom and her sisters and brothers were all very close. We lived in a small town in lower Delaware for years. Mom and Aunt Patsy, her next eldest sister, always lived close together in the same town in the early years when I was growing up. These two were almost inseparable. I remember when we had an apartment up on the hill and my Aunt Patsy lived right next door. She had three children during that time, and we all did almost everything together.

We had other family too who didn't live far away, including my grandmother Della who lived around the corner. I loved walks to her house to visit. She had the cutest little pink house on Coulter Street. She always had a garden that she tended to, and my uncles would come by to help her keep it up and would bring vegetables from their garden.

I didn't know my grandfather Othar, as he passed away from Leukemia when my mother was little. We were a big family who stay closed to one another. Gatherings in the summer were always fun and a great time to see everybody and enjoy good southern food. My aunties all could cook, and each had their own specialty food.

When we moved after living with my uncle for a while, Mom had purchased her first mobile home in Ellendale. Ellendale is a very small town with one stoplight back then and still one stoplight today. It seemed all our family lived there already by the time we moved. Mom's sisters and brothers stayed within miles from one another in this small town just as we had in Milton.

I was excited about this move, as I got to see my cousins every day again. We moved two houses down from Aunt Patsy, and Aunt Aggie lived right beside her. We were all together again.

I attended church at a young age, going to my grandmother's church where she lived, but when we moved, my cousins and I started going to Mt. Zion African Methodist Episcopal Church attending the Sunday school classes. We would load up in Mom's, Aunt Aggie's, or Aunt Patsy's car—whoever was taking us to drop us off. I enjoyed the classes and learned a lot from my first Sunday school teacher. After Sunday school, we would walk down to the corner store and buy candy with any money we had left over that we didn't put in the collection plate at church or spending money we were given for doing chores around the house. We all looked forward to that.

Mom raised her children as a single mother, not receiving

child support for any them. I don't recall many men in my mom's life but two. My father, the late Hilbert Watson was nonexistent in my life during the early years. He wasn't one of the two. I didn't get to know him until I was in my early thirties. My mom didn't have anything to say about him good or bad. I do recall her telling me that I was the product of a one-night stand and that she wasn't a willing participant. I had to think about that for a minute, as it stunned me when she first said it. I was curious what Hilbert had to say about that. When I questioned my father, he said that wasn't how he remembered it but didn't elaborate on it either. I didn't push the issue. It didn't really matter. I was here regardless of how it happened—not much anyone could do about it now. I just know that mom always made me feel loved.

I did spend a couple of summers with my father and his family. He was married and lived in Maryland with three children. That's when I learned I had another little brother. Hilbert was a military policemen in the US Army. He had come around to see me a few times after the summer visits until the promises that he was coming turned into something he wasn't following through on. Even then, my mom still didn't speak badly about him, but whenever he did come around after not showing up, she let him know it wasn't cool. Mom was truly being mother and father to me and my siblings.

The gentleman Mom was very fond of was Christopher Green, who was my youngest brother's father. Chris lived in Pennsylvania and would come to visit on the weekends. He bought me my first watch, taught me how to drive a car, and would always give me money to buy books at school. I didn't understand why he only came around on the weekends but at first I figured it was from the long drive. One day he and Mom were having a disagreement. I was listening outside the door when I heard Mom tell him that she didn't want to see him anymore because it wasn't right, and it wasn't right because now she was going to church and trying to get her life in order. Chris didn't seem to take it well and insisted he wasn't going anywhere. I knew that was a decision that was hard for Mom to make, but she did and stuck by it. She won the disagreement.

I remember Chris from most of my childhood and loved him just like he was my own father. When Mom ended things, not only did he not take it well; I didn't either. He would still come to visit after that day but spent the night sleeping in the chair in the living room chain-smoking cigarettes. He would try to make his way in the bedroom to see her, but she wasn't having it and asked him to leave. One day he stopped coming around like he was before, but he did call and came to visit his son, my youngest brother Timmy.

Mom continued going to church more and embraced her new life of serving the Lord. She was saved and happy. She always loved to sing and had a beautiful alto voice. She started singing at church with her sisters, brother, and brother-in-law in a group they called the Voices of Hope. They would travel to different churches singing as a family group. On the weekends, they all get together to practice.

Mom really enjoyed being a part of the group. Later, my sister and cousin joined them too.

One day we got the news that Chris was sick and had been diagnosed with lung cancer. Although Mom had ended the relationship, she still cared about Chris. She always said he was the love of her life. Mom wanted to go see him, so my sister and I went with her. Chris looked so frail as we walked into the room. He couldn't speak through his oxygen mask, but he knew we were there. I watched Mom as she sat beside his bed and rested her hand on top of his hand. Missy and I walked out of the room to give them privacy.

Chris was the only male I was around beside my older brother when I was growing up. Although he wasn't perfect over the years, he treated me well, as if I were his own daughter. As I looked at him lying quietly in the hospital bed, the memories came back and reminded me again how much I appreciated his visits and all that he had done for me. It was heartbreaking to see him lying there. I didn't know that would be the last time I would see him. He looked thin and tired. I kissed him on his forehead. We all said a prayer before leaving.

A few weeks after our visit, Chris passed away. My mom didn't go to the funeral out of respect for his wife and other sons but planned for my little brother to attend with his cousin Patsy. My brother Timmy looks a lot like his dad, so I see Chris every time I see him. There's a picture of Chris and Mom that some say looks a lot like Timmy and me.

CHAPTER 2

ROUND ONE— THE C WORD

My kids grew up around Mom and loved spending time with their grandmother. The family closeness we felt growing up continued when we started our own family. We enjoyed the time we spent together. Family was what we knew. We would all visit Mom frequently on the weekends and always for the holidays.

The kids and I were living in Dover when Mom was first diagnosed with cancer back in 1990. She went to her doctor to have a mammogram done, which is how she found out that there was a lump. Mom had to have a wedge of her breast removed. It wasn't good news, and it was hard for her to tell the family about it. She had told her sisters, and they were all very supportive.

The doctor had explained to her what she needed to do next. She started taking medication that she would have to take for five years. Once she had the surgery to remove the cancer, she was headed toward remission. It was a blessing, and we thought at the time that all the cancer had been removed. Slowing life as she knew it seemed to be a little more normal. She kept up with her appointments and took her medicine as prescribed, following the doctor's orders perfectly. She was very conscientious of that.

Mom had gone back to work and seemed adjusted after everything she had gone through. She had to wear special mastectomy bras. Mom never complained about how she looked. I often wondered what her thoughts were about her body, but we didn't talk about it. We made sure that she had the garments she needed and that she was comfortable wearing them. Still, being the strong, God-fearing women she was, it was not surprise to me that she had survived that first diagnose. Mom was a fighter in every way. She was winning!

One day my mom called me before she was leaving to go into work. She was going to stop by to see me before I left to go to Dover, as there was a bill she wanted me to pay. She never stopped by, and I assumed she had run out of time. When I got to work, I received a call that Mom had been in an accident. Another car had hit her from the side, which caused her car to roll over twice. She was rushed to the hospital. I was so worried and quickly left to go see her.

Mom was plenty shaken up from the accident. She was trembling when she told me what happened as if it was happening to her all over again. She was driving her Ford station wagon when another vehicle didn't stop at the intersection on the back road she was traveling to come see me. The driver plowed into the side of her car. It was amazing that she got out of the car with only a sprained arm, cuts, and bruises considering how her car looked. It was totaled! Mom knew how blessed she was and thanked God consistently that she survived—first cancer and now this car accident.

Driving with Mom after that was a little interesting, as she jumped at stops and turns and wasn't comfortable to drive on her own for some time. She would make motions to stop even though she wasn't the one driving. Eventually, she gained control of her anxiety about driving and was back on the road. Mom finally purchased another car, and again, her life was getting back to normal. She had even returned to work.

CHAPTER 3

THE POWER OF
FORGIVENESS!

The other love that found Mom was a gentleman named Robert Harris. Mom lived alone after we all grew up and left. Then one day when I stopped by for my regular weekend visit there was a man at the house. He looked like he had been sitting for a while and seemed to be pleasant as he spoke to the kids and me as we walked in. I was pleasantly surprised and sort of gave Mom the eye like, *What's going on here?* Mom told me that I knew this man, as he was neighbor's son who lived next door. I couldn't quite place him at first, but he did look familiar. He seemed friendly enough, but I couldn't help but wonder when he started visiting. As time went on, we found out that Robert was visiting Mom more frequently. She seemed to enjoy his company.

Robert and Mom got married in December 1992. She was so excited about getting married. We planned her day! On the day of the wedding, my sister and I helped her get ready. Her jet-black hair was pulled back, and her smooth, bronze skin was radiant. The red lipstick accented her perfectly straight teeth when she smiled. Standing five six in her white wedding dress with matching white pumps, she looked absolutely stunning.

I could see her looking back at herself in the mirror. Our eyes met, and I nodded, saying, "The dress fits you perfectly, Mom!" She wore my wedding dress and looked beautiful. I've never been so happy for her as I was on that day. She was there for me when I got married, and now I was there for her when she got married. Mom needed some happiness in her life, as losing my brother took a toll on her. Missy, Timmy, and I were present along with her mom, sisters, and best friend, Maggie.

The wedding was at Mom's home where she and Robert resided after they were married for nine years. From the beginning, I could see how much they loved one another. Robert was always attentive to her needs and would do anything for her. Her Boaz finally found her.

After losing my oldest brother, Gregory, when he was twenty-eight, I was grateful that Mom had someone in her life, so she didn't have to spend days alone. I often worried about her, but when she married Robert, I felt some relieve that she would be okay. Although nothing could replace the loss of my brother in her life he would help fill the void of missing her son. Mom didn't talk about it much but I knew the loneliness of not having Greg around broke her heart.

Greg had schizophrenia and had walked into someone's apartment who then rustled with him, and he ended up with a fatal stab wound to his heart. This was a great loss to our family. Mom would say that she didn't ever want to bury any of her children, as it should be the other way around. I saw how heartbroken my mom was. Greg was her firstborn and oldest son. That was when I first witnessed just how strong of a woman she was during tragedy. I never once heard her swear or raise her voice or say anything negative about the situation. She didn't question God. She cried and was distraught; however, she took it in stride and comforted us.

Mom always remembered his birthday and the day be passed away by lighting a candle. Dealing with my brother's murder was hard, having to accept not only that he was gone but how he died violently. Despite that, my mom didn't hold a grudge against the man who took his life. She had questions and concerns; we all did. There were a couple of different stories surrounding the incident and how he died, but Mom made her peace with it. I was astounded by that.

Mom reminded me about forgiveness. That was very important to her. She always said you must be able to forgive just as God forgave us for our sins. When you forgive, you release the power for someone else to hold it over you. When you offer that person forgiveness, you release the hold he or she has over you. You offer forgiveness for the other person as well as yourself. That was my first lesson learned about forgiveness in a big way.

I am not sure what made me want to find the person who killed my brother, but I found him while he was still in the hospital. I didn't speak at first when he answered the phone, but I finally told him my name and who I was. Surprisingly, he didn't hang up, as I imagine I would have if I were him. He instantly started to cry profusely, apologizing and stating he didn't have a choice. I could barely understand what he was saying. He kept repeating that he didn't have a choice. He told me his little daughter was in the house and said he had to protect his family. He kept apologizing and said he was sorry. I don't know if he was sincere, but it sounded like it. I could hear the guilt and the regret in his voice.

No charges were filed because the police said he had a right to protect himself in his own home. My brother was the intruder. I knew from talking with him that this would be something that would haunt him for the rest of his life. I was certain no punishment would take away what he was feeling.

I told him that I forgave him. I meant it. I was hurt and sad about all of it. I quickly remembered what Mom had told me about forgiveness. I know some people wouldn't understand that conversation, and part of me didn't. I felt it was the right thing to do.

I was emotional when I told Mom about the conversation.

She was surprised I had found him and had spoken to him.

She said, "Yes, we have to be able to forgive. It's okay."

We never spoke about it again after that.

CHAPTER 4

~

ROUND TWO— IT'S BACK!

It was five years later when the cancer came back. Mom was no longer in remission. This part of Mom's journey in her life was one that I didn't understand. I just couldn't comprehend why someone so loving, so faithful, and with such a strong trust in God had to encounter this battle with cancer *again*. I felt there were so many other bad people in the world; surely, she should have been one to be spared. Why was this happening? I had a lot of questions, and God had some explaining to do!

I remember when my sister and I got the call to go see Mom. We were all disappointed to hear her explain to us that the cancer had come back. I didn't know what to do with this bad news again. We sat with her, we cried, and we hugged her. She explained that she was going to do what the doctors said and trust that everything was going to be okay.

She had to take chemotherapy. I knew she believed that, but I questioned it. Where these the same doctors who thought they got all the cancer before when she had a wedge of her breast removed? After seeing the look on her face, I couldn't have an outburst at that time. She meant every word of what she was saying to us. I just felt numb and helpless.

That was my first feeling of absolute rage. I didn't know what to do or what to say, but I knew it was best for her to follow her lead, as this was one of the most difficult things she had to tell us again. Mom was comforting us. She told us that no one knows how much time anyone has and that we would see what happens. We had to trust God. She was amazing because at that time all I wanted to do was to curse at God.

I absolutely cherish those quiet moments I had with Mom during her final months. She was incredible. I saw her to be so brave as she prepared our family for her departure, not once thinking of herself. Right from the onset, she was firm with her expectations and acceptance. From the time she told us about the diagnosis to when she took her last breath, she was consistent with her message. That totally amazed me and still does until this day—what amazing grace.

The strength I find within myself comes from what Mom taught me and, more importantly, what she showed me. It's how I learned to be selfless. Nothing I had experienced in my life prepared me for the pain I experienced losing my mother. Although I knew it was coming, I went through all the stages of being in denial, angry, withdrawn, and finally accepting. Each stage was brutal and filled with overwhelming emotion.

As time went on, Mom wanted to spend as much time with her five grandchildren as she could. She didn't get to meet her great-grandchildren, but I know she would have loved them just as much too. Our last Christmas holiday was fun and filled with all the food we could eat. That gathering was the best with everyone present to enjoy one another. Our family gatherings were not the same after that holiday. My sister and I stayed close and kept our families closer when Mom was sick.

Although we knew Mom was sick and the doctors did all they could to help prepare her and our family to understand that her sickness was incurable, I just wasn't ready to accept it. They tried to explain we had time, but that was not resonating with me at all. I was in total denial that one day I would not have my mom here on Earth. I did not stop to think or consider that the time they spoke of was a gift and needed to be cherished. I tried to understand it but couldn't. We lost my brother, and now I was being told we were going to one day lose Mom too.

When Mom got sick, I was very much involved in church. I still remember her laughing when I told her that I wanted to study under the pastor to be a minister. I reckon she knew my hellion ways I had growing up and thought it wasn't something I was serious about doing. But I did it! At that point in my life, I had never been closer to God than I was just before finding out that Mom's cancer had returned. Little did I know how much my faith was going to be tested.

My family and I attended Harvest for The World Ministries every Sunday. Having grown up in the church,

I really wanted my kids to know and have a spiritual relationship with God. I always taught them that no one was perfect, but we live our lives with integrity, loving and helping others. It was important to me that they saw me live my life that way. I believe children emulate what they see, and I wanted to be the best example for them. I chose that church because that's where my mom fellowshipped along with my aunts and uncle. It was a treat to see all of them on Sunday and go to their homes after church for a home-cooked meal. It was the best part of my Sunday.

Mom was greatly missed when she stopped being able to attend church. That's when the reality first started to hit me that one day we were going to lose her. We started to see what the doctors told us to expect. I started thinking about her all the time. I tried to find scripture to comfort me at first. One in particular reads: "To be absent from the body means to be present with the Lord" (2 Corinthians 5:8 KJV). It made me think about where others I loved and who had passed away were.

With everything that Mom was going through, I wanted to do something to help lift her spirits. It had to be something that would show her how much she was loved and appreciated. She deserved to have some happiness after fighting cancer the first time, after the accident, and now having the fight continue. I thought it would be great to have an appreciation dinner in her honor.

I ran the idea by my family, and we all agreed it would be perfect. We planned the event at a church hall not far from where Mom lived. Her sisters told her they were going to someone's birthday celebration and wanted her to attend. Luckily, she agreed.

On the day of the event, the room was decorated, there was food and desserts prepared, there was music playing, and guest arrived ahead of time as requested. We then waited for the honoree to arrive.

Words can't express the joy I felt when she walked in and realized the surprise was for her. I think we scared he a little when we yelled *surprise*! She became emotional very quickly. I put my arms around her and let her know that everyone was there to celebrate and appreciate her. We sat her in the front of the room as the queen she was.

As everyone sat around chatting and chewing, it was time to for family and friends to recognize Mom. As person after person shared their most prideful moments, she sat and quietly cried as she wiped her tears away, although more filled the more she listened. Mom couldn't help but be caught up in the moment. The words that were shared and the songs that were sung in her presence meant everything to her. She was overjoyed, and I know that was a moment she would never forget. Mission accomplished!

CHAPTER 5

THE PREPARATION

I remember that when Mom started going to chemotherapy, I started praying endlessly that she would kick cancer's butt. As time went on, the negative shift in my attitude progressed, and I found myself mad and angry as hell at God. I just couldn't understand why He would allow this to happen to someone like Mom who was so devoted to what she believed and had so much trust in God. She was dedicated and always trusted and believed in the Bible. I believed that if you worry there's no need to pray and if you pray there's no need to worry. I worried and prayed all the time until I couldn't.

I didn't stop going to church, but my heart wasn't in it like it had been before. And the closer we got to losing Mom, the more apparent my withdrawal became. The faith I thought I'd had turned into doubt. My emotions during those days got the best of me. I couldn't talk about it and tried not to think about it. It drained me! I was able to hide it better on some days than others. Damn cancer! We sent a man to the moon, but there's still no cure for cancer. I know Mom had accepted it, but I didn't. I couldn't. I wouldn't! She still didn't question it or ask why. I probably did that enough for the both of us. Every day was a gift to her, and she saw and embraced it as such.

My stepfather told me when she first found out that the cancer was back, someone from the doctor's office had come to the house to explain everything to them and walk them through the formalities. They were told that no time could be given when it would happen, as it could be a week or months, but what was known for sure was that it was going to happen. They both cried. And after the nurse left, my stepfather and mom talked. He said they cried again and even then, almost immediately, she started worrying about him. She told him to get himself right and not to be scared. She said she was going to be all right. The next step was to let her family know. That touched my heart! Where did she get this humble spirit from? To her, it was always about her family. She wasn't worried about herself.

I remembered playing the conversation with her repeatedly in my head when she told me that the cancer had come back. She said that she would do whatever she needed to do, but when the time came, she wanted me to strong and not to worry about her. I went to her doctors' appointments looking for answers, and they explained that the cancer had started to spread. There was no explanation as to why. They just knew it was back.

Later, after finding out the cancer had returned, it eventually became inflammatory breast cancer. The nipple started to invert on her remaining breast, and she complained of a burning sensation. I watched her go through this again, more devastating than the first time. I couldn't imagine what she was feeling.

Mom didn't talk about how she felt emotionally, and

honestly, I was too scared to ask because I knew I wouldn't be able to handle it. I was scared that I wouldn't be able to provide the comfort she needed because I was so damn angry! Mom said she missed having her breast, but it was okay. It was going to happen, and nothing she could do would change it.

The cancer then spread to her brain, and she started taking stereotactic radiation to try isolating the cancer from spreading further. It wasn't successful, and the radiation treatment had to be stopped. She had reached a point where radiation was no longer an option.

How I wish … I would give anything to have her here now to talk to her and share with her all the great things that are happening in my life, how our family has grown and how all the things she told me would happen did.

Mom went out of her way to prepare everyone around her. When she tried to talk to me about it, I was anything but receptive and would shut down. At one point, I stopped going home to see her and made excuses that there was something else I had to do. We still talked on the phone every day. I know she knew I was delaying coming to see her, as weekend visits were our routine. Now I would give anything to visit again.

Our last words after every conversation were, "I love you!" Even when we didn't talk for long, we connected daily. There was one day she called me and asked me to come see her. I knew it was important to her, as I could hear it in her voice. She was always worried about how I was doing, and I would remind her not to worry about me, that I was fine. She saw through that for sure. Mom would always tell me that she knew it was hard for me to accept, but I had to carry on and be strong. She would say things like, "I am always going to be with you. You must be strong for your family. They are going to need you, and I need you to be there for them."

Mom didn't let cancer be the big elephant in the room. She would say the silliest things to make others laugh. I remember when she lost all her hair and it grew back jet-black, curly, and beautiful. She would say, "What else would make that happen? Now I don't even need a perm. I have good curly hair! I even have my baby hair back! Look at God!" Her laugh was infectious, and eventually, she would make me laugh too.

From the beginning, I had hoped Mom would have opted to have both breasts removed to keep the cancer from spreading, but she didn't want to do that and lose both breasts. I never asked her if she wished she had done that, and she never mentioned it. She was always adamant about not wanting to be cut on. She wanted to do things on her own terms. She would say, "My time is my time! I trust God!"

I went to as many more doctor's appointments with Mom and my stepfather as I could. When Mom stopped working, I knew that was hard because she loved to keep busy, I was very thankful for my stepfather, as he took great care of her when she was sick. He stuck by my mom's side through everything, and when she couldn't get around and do things for herself, we would make sure to be there to help him and ensure had had time to himself. I knew he appreciated that time. This was hard on him, but he too was always concerned about how I was doing. My conversations with him were always encouraging. He knew that this was something I was having trouble accepting, and my guess was Mom probably told him too.

Robert called me one day to tell me that she needed to talk to me and that she was worried about me. That's when I realized I was acting selfish. Amazing … She was the one fighting for her life, and she was worried about me. That was a burden I didn't want to put on her, considering everything she was going through.

I felt so ashamed of my behavior and had to quickly change it. It wasn't about me. It was about her, and it was time that I started to act like it. I thought about how much time I had wasted not taking every advantage of time to spend with her and show her I would be okay. That was what she needed to see. Now I get it. It was time for me to suck it up and do all that I could to make the time left with Mom the best time for her and for our family.

I went with Mom and Robert to the last appointment when the doctor told us what to expect from that point on and explained that she couldn't take any more radiation treatment.

Mom sat quietly and nodded her head and said, "Thank you, Doctor. I know you have done all you can." She smiled at the doctor.

When Mom and Robert walked out, I stayed behind. I stood there and couldn't really find the words to say anything. I looked at the doctor, and she held my hand. She didn't say anything. As I looked at her with tears running down my face, she said, "I've never seen anyone take the news of their diagnosis as bravely as your mother. I am praying for her and your family."

I agreed and left the office.

When I got to the car, my mom looked at me and smiled. She whispered, "It's going to be okay. I am going to be okay. It's in God's hands now. I don't want you to worry about me. Okay?"

I hugged her so tightly. As I watched them drive off, I sat there in the car so astounded at the strength my mom had even in that moment. I didn't know how she was doing it. I never saw her upset—not even once—about what was happening to her. I was still falling apart, but I knew I had to get it together and keep it together. The tears just wouldn't stop flowing. I reminded myself again and promised that I would get in as much time and be there for whatever it was she needed or wanted to do.

My visits to see Mom were more frequent, and I enjoyed our time talking and laughing together. Whenever I walked into the room saying, "Hey, beautiful lady!" she would always smile back at me. That beautiful smile lit up her face! Mom continued to read the Bible when she could and watch the religious channels on television. I would read to her too. She really loved that when she tired easily. Many times, she would fall asleep while I was reading.

I remember just sitting and watching her and thinking about all the wonderful moments in time with her: My childhood memories. How that one day when my sister was running from her and my mom caught her. That was hilarious! All three times when she was with me when I had my children. Showing her how to use the big dinosaur cell phone when they first came out. When she attended my high school graduation. When I got married the second time, and she said, "Let's make this the last time." All the family gatherings with her sister and brothers. Her wedding. And the sad times when she lost Greg and when her mom passed.

It was a lifetime of precious memories. There were more great times than bad. I just couldn't think about life without her. I started thinking about what she would miss and what I was going to miss: when the kids get married, grandkids having kids of their own, weddings and graduations to come. We would all miss her presence. Then I thought about how I would go on not talking to her every day. Coming to see her and finding her if she wasn't home. How would I handle not hearing her voice, not being able to tell her about my day and hearing about hers, and not telling her I loved her? Who would call me on my birthday and sing to me?

There is no one like your mother. No one will ever be able to replace her. Mom framed me to be the women I am today. Mom wasn't perfect, but she was perfect to me. Of all her children, I do feel like I was the most like her.

I watched her raise my sister, my two brothers, and me with no help from our fathers. She made sure we had food to eat, clothes to wear, and a place to lay our heads. We didn't have fancy things or wear designer clothes, but we had one another, and we had the love of our mother. Mom was our sole provider. I watched how she managed her life and learned so much from her. She was independent.

I remember when she told me there were two things in her lifetime that she regretted, and when she accepted Jesus as her Savior, they were forgiven. She was a new creature. She would say that's when her blessings really started. A few years later when she married Robert, she didn't think she would ever get married but she did. She wore the wedding dress I got married in, and Mom looked amazing. Mom was excited about overcoming her mistakes and how God still loved her despite them.

During all the craziness that was happening, Mom still had a positive attitude and faith beyond anything I could understand. I gained so much strength from watching her. She was selfless and worried about others more than herself right up until she left us. Mom was so giving and didn't ask for anything in return. She was not only a beautiful woman on the outside, but that beauty shined from the inside, which made her totally radiant. I can hear saying, "I'm not perfect, but Jesus loves me and you!" She would tell me that time and time again. Mom believed God had washed away her sin, and she was all in from that point on. She lived her life by example and was humble about everything in her life—the good and the bad.

~

CHAPTER 6

WHEN GOD CLEANS YOU UP

In the last few months, it became extremely hard to see Mom go through the final stages of having cancer. The changes were more noticeable. When she lost her hair, it grew back in more beautiful than it was before. One night my sister and I were sitting at the table talking with her. On this day, Mom was different. She looked different too. I always thought she was beautiful, but this day something about her glowed. There was something luminous about her. To look at her in that moment, you would not have known she was battling anything that threatened her life.

It was hard for Mom to sit up for long periods of time. She wanted to get dressed and put clothes on rather than wear her nightgown. We got her into her pink sweat suit. She asked if I could do her face, not that I was really got at it, but she always liked when I would arch her eyebrows. She also requested a little makeup. This seemed to make her smile, so I was happy and quick to do it. I got her makeup from the bathroom, and she sat at the table as if this were just an ordinary day. I gently put on lipstick, eyeliner, and mascara and then arched her eyebrows and smeared a little blush on her cheeks. She always loved red lipstick. I used my tube to finish the look. I handed her the mirror, and in Aunt Aggie's voice, I said "Just gorgeous!" The three of us laughed. She really did look amazing. I got the camera and took her picture. It's one of my favorite pictures of her. Even when I look at the picture now, I recall that moment like it was yesterday. I'll never forget it. We all truly enjoyed that time. It was great to see her sitting up talking, laughing, and smiling. It's hard to believe that Mom passed away a week later. I saw firsthand what the old folks say: "God cleans you up before He takes you." That day was significant because she looked better than she ever had before. You couldn't see the impact that cancer had made in her appearance at all.

The thought of trying to prepare myself to let Mom go grew more and more unbearable, but I worked hard to not let it show to anyone. After our visits in person or talking on the phone, I would just cry and laugh thinking about all the good times and moments we had and were making. I just wanted her to be at peace and happy. She continued trying to prepare the family for what was going to happen by showing and telling us she was okay.

After she passed, I found out that she had specific conversations with all of us on what she expected us to do. She told my then husband to make sure he took care of her girl. She was telling me and those around me to look after one another. Whenever she needed to see me, she'd have my stepfather call to check on me and ask me to come by so she could see for herself. I truly struggled with that because I knew what the conversation was going to be about. It had gotten to the point that when I went to see Mom I wouldn't stay that long. It was just so tough. I didn't consider again how my actions would be affecting her. She told me she understood why I had stayed away. It was so hard for me to cope.

I had to be honest with her when we met that day. I explained to her that I didn't know how to let go. I told her I was afraid of losing her. A part of me was mad with her that she wasn't angry. Deep down inside, I felt like she wasn't fighting hard enough, but I knew she was. It was wrong for me to judge her, but it was how I felt. She told me that she had accepted having cancer a time long ago. She said she was mad and upset, but it wasn't going to change anything. It was more important for her to love her family and know that we would be okay and prepared when the time came. She told me to be happy and take care of myself when she was gone and to keep God first in all that I do. Right there and then, those words stung. I didn't say it out loud, but I was not feeling the idea to "keep God first!" But, I kept my promise and spent as much time with her as I could, and I stopped judging. Mom was the one fighting for her life. She was fighting her way on her own terms. I was fighting to hold on to her, and she was fighting to prepare me to let go.

Mom explained to me how she felt when she lost my grandmother and that she understood what I was feeling. That's why she was trying so hard to help me understand. She said she would get to see her mom again one day and that I would get to see her too when she leaves this life, but I had to keep the faith.

About a month before Mom's birthday, I had taken a leave of absence from work to spend more time with her. She had gotten to the point that she wasn't able to walk on her own or do things for herself without help. My oldest daughter, Tynisha, would go and sit with her and help care for her during the day with my stepfather. He was amazing during this time, sticking beside his wife the entire time. I was so very appreciative that he honored his vows for richer or poorer and in sickness or health. My sister, aunts, and I would be there as much as possible to help care for Mom. Additional support was coming in to help to cover the gaps when Robert was at work. He never once complained or asked anyone for anything. Whatever Mom needed, he attended to and ensured it was done.

Mom gave us all a scare the day she fell through the coffee table in the living room. It was hard for her to accept help, as she was a proud woman and still tried to do things on her own. We were thankful that the table had more damage than she did, but it terrified her enough to allow others to help her.

We went to Mom's last doctor's appointment when we were told the time was getting close. Now was the time to call the family in to come see her. This was hard. Hospice had started coming to assist. Things got very real, very quickly.

My sister started to call the family to let them know it was time to come see Mom, as she wasn't getting better.

I sat in the room with her holding her hand as my aunts, uncles, cousins, and friends started coming to visit her. At times, she was awake and could see people, but other times, she was resting. They would hug her and tell her how much they loved her. I don't know if she knew that for many of them, this would be the last time she would see them.

I was dying inside, as I still couldn't believe this was happening. I have never felt so helpless in all my life as I did at that moment. People would tell me to be strong and offer their condolence. They would say things like, "It's going to be okay. We're praying for you. It's in God's hands." Some didn't know what to say and would just hug me. I was just so angry all over again! I just sat there because I didn't want Mom to be alone. No matter what happened, I was going to be with her until the end. I started thinking about the song she used to sing: "I Come to the Garden Alone."

CHAPTER 7

~

LAST BIRTHDAY

My mom was approaching her sixtieth birthday. During this week, she had started sleeping a whole lot more. She was coherent when she was awake. We would sit and talk with her if she wanted to talk, or we would read to her. My aunts would sing songs, and we played gospel music. Mom started having more seizures, and the medication she was taking helped keep her stay sedated. My sister and I stayed with her at the house that last week of her birthday. My aunties and stepfather were there. She wasn't sitting up on her own anymore.

The day before her birthday, she told me she was proud of me and that she loved me. She told me to be sure to take good care of myself. She talked about her husband and making sure he took care of himself too. The next thing she said tore me to pieces, and I cried as I held her hand. I read her favorite verse "But they that wait upon the Lord shall renew their strength; they shall mount up with wings as eagles; they shall run, and not be weary; and they shall walk, and not faint" (Isaiah 40:31 KJV).

She looked up at me and said, "When's my birthday?"

I said, "It's tomorrow, Mom. You're almost there."

She smiled and said with such calmness, "I am ready to go home."

Tears fell down her face, and I wiped them as she smiled back at me. I wanted to tell her to not talk like that, but I know she knew the time was getting close. When I looked into her eyes, I didn't see someone who was afraid or scared. There was a peace that I hadn't quite seen before. She truly was waiting on the Lord, and she was ready!

That night it was hard to fall asleep. I would sit up and just pray that God wouldn't take her. If ever there was a miracle I was praying for, this was it. I was desperate to keep her here with us much longer than the short time we had. There was so much more time that I wanted—that I needed. She was such a force in my life—in our family's lives. I couldn't begin to imagine what life would be like not being able to call and talk with her every day. She would always say that we never know when our last breath would be, so be sure to say I love you. If it was close to midnight and I hadn't spoken with her, I would call her or she would call me. That was our thing. I couldn't lose her.

The time was approaching too fast, and I wasn't prepared to say goodbye. I couldn't. My attitude changed quickly. That rage I was feeling before was back. I was bitter. I couldn't pray. I didn't want to talk. I just wanted Mom to live.

When she woke up the next day, I sang "Happy Birthday" and ended with that favorite part she always sang to me on my birthday. "Have I told you lately how much I love you?"

She smiled and said, "I made it."

I sat beside her and listened as she tried to sing. Her voice was now a subtle whisper. She was trying to sing "I Come to the Garden Alone."

Yes, she had finally made it to see her sixtieth birthday.

It was a milestone that we all wanted to celebrate, but she didn't have the strength to participate now. I read the Bible to her until she fell asleep that night. As I looked at her sleeping, I thought about all the times she would be the first one to call me on my birthday to sing "Happy Birthday," adding, "Have I told you lately how much I love you?" She never missed my birthday, and I always looked forward to hearing her sing that song.

More company came over to see her throughout the day on her birthday, but she wasn't much company, as she was sleeping most of the time. We all sat and talked in the living room and checked in on Mom often to make sure she was comfortable. Holding full conversations was starting to become nonexistent, but she would open her eyes and push through with a smile.

The seizures started happening even more frequently. She wasn't coherent most of the time at this point when we were talking to her. I sat by her side as everyone came in her room to hug and kiss her, knowing this was probably the last time they would have the opportunity to do so. I felt like the days were long and standing still, but I know that was all in my mind. I was afraid of what was going to happen next. I could see how things were changing for Mom, and her health was continuing to decline.

How could someone so innocent who loved God so much with all her heart be still preparing me for that moment when she would no longer be here with me? Mom was so strong right to the very end. The very last thing she said to me and that I said to her was, "I love you." It was what we always did before we got off the phone or left one another's presence. I still do that with my loved ones today, and I miss hearing my mom's voice telling me that every day.

The last seizure Mom had at the house was severe. I called the doctor, and she recommended we take her to the hospital. We called the ambulance, and she was admitted.

Before leaving the house, as I stood in her bedroom, I knew that when she was taken to the hospital she wouldn't be coming back to her home again. I had a void already starting to fill my spirit. I picked up her Bible and held it for a minute. As I walked out the door, it was sunny. I looked up and remember thinking, *It's your will, God.*

CHAPTER 8

~

BITTERSWEET MOMENT

Our family was at the hospital when the doctor arrived and told us that all that could be done now was to keep Mom comfortable. She was still breathing on her own, but it was very shallow. Mom was in the hospital for a day and a half, and I stayed with her, as I didn't want her to be alone. She never woke up again, but I held onto the last words she said to me.

Robert and the aunties were in the room when the nurse came in to check her. I was sitting by Mom's bedside, waiting for my sister to come back into the room. I sat holding her hand, which started feeling cold. I remember thinking my sister needed to be there. The nurse had come back in the room again. She looked at me, and I looked down over at Mom as she took her last breath. It was 1:58 p.m. when the heart monitor flatlined.

The nurse said, "I'm so sorry. She's gone." The nurse left the room to give us time to say goodbye.

Mom passed on June 19, 2001, three days after her birthday. When my sister came back into the room, I didn't have to say anything, as the look around the room spoke for what just had happened. We all kissed her one last time.

When everyone left the room, I stayed behind. I wasn't ready to leave her yet. I just sat there a few moments, wanting to talk to her. I tried to pray, but the words wouldn't come. I kissed her hand again. When the nurse came back, she asked me if we wanted to keep her jewelry. I nodded yes. She removed the wedding ring and mother's ring from her hand and handed them to me. Robert was standing in the doorway waiting for me. I couldn't believe this moment had come, but it had. We stood there as the nurse removed Mom from the machine. She was gone, and how sweet she looked lying there asleep. I touched my mom one last time and kissed her forehead before leaving. I dreaded this day! Now that it was here, it all felt so surreal.

I had that feeling of emptiness again, and the void was larger than life. But out of nowhere, I stopped and began to pray again. It was the bittersweet moment I hadn't anticipated. I asked God to please take care of Mom and asked that her soul would rest forever in His arms.

I remember thinking, *What am I going to do next?* And it was clear. I would do what Mom had asked me to do. I would do what she prepared me to do. I was going to be strong. I was going to be okay.

Flash after flash of her amazing life and her laughter all flooded my mind, coming back to me. I was honored to be able to sit beside her until the end. As she lay so still with a peaceful look on her face, I was wondering what she was experiencing in her last moments. Could she hear me? Did she see flashes of her life before she slipped away too?

Still beautiful, she was my mother! She was with me when I came into this world, and I was with her when she left. I knew she loved me unconditionally, as I did her. I thought about all the great times we had together. I was so thankful for all the memories. And those memories were flooding back so fast I almost laughed out loud … bittersweet, bittersweet. Although my heart was breaking, I knew she was no longer suffering, and she was going where she wanted to be. I could hear her telling me again she was ready to go home. She went home. She won.

The time finally came when we were all back at the house for the first time without Mom. It was quiet at first, awkward even. I went back to my mom's room and sat there. I looked around the room at her things and held the pillow that she had laid her head on. My sister came in and sat beside me. We hugged in silence. She told me again it was going to be okay and that we had one another. I appreciated that. I think we grew even closer after Mom passed away. No way could I ever replace the void in my life losing my Mom. Having my sister now was everything. Before I left to go home, I hugged Robert extra tight. I knew it would be hard for him being in the house by himself now without Mom. I thought it to be unbearable to be alone and offered to stay, but he said he was going to be all right.

Over the next few days after Mom passed, we had to plan the funeral. I didn't go to the funeral home to help handle the details, as I wasn't ready for that. My sister and cousin handled that along with Robert. My sister and I picked out what she was going to wear. Blue was Mom's favorite color, and we choose a blue suit with a white blouse. I had her rings placed on her fingers again. She wore the two rings that meant everything to her: her wedding ring and her mother's ring.

The day of the funeral, we all met at Mom's house. We also choose to wear blue and white. I recall just sitting and listening to people talk. My kids were close by me, checking to make sure I was okay. The car arrived, and we all headed to the church for the going home celebration. We all walked in as a family and were seated in the front row. We viewed Mom one last time before closing the casket.

As I sat and listened to the singing and kind words of clergy and friends, all I could think about was wanting to go home. This was a lot to endure, but I managed to get through the service. When it was time for the procession out, I kneeled on the altar to pray. I asked God for strength to help me and my family to get through the days ahead, as we couldn't do it on our own. I also asked for forgiveness in questioning Him.

We all met at the grave site for the burial and went back to the church hall for the repast. Things just didn't feel the same without Mom. I didn't stay the whole time and headed back home. If I received one more hug or sad look, I was going to explode. It took everything in me not to scream out loud. It was nice to see a lot of family I hadn't seen in a while but wished it was under better circumstances. Right now, it was time for me to go. It was starting to feel hard to breathe.

Now that everything was done, many of my thoughts continued to take over thinking about Mom. They were good thoughts. It was good for me mentally to let go of the anger. I had to learn to follow my own advice that I had given to others and take one day at a time. It is important to allow yourself time to grieve. Go with the feelings. If you need to laugh, laugh, or if you need to cry, cry. If you need to sit still, sit still, and if you need to scream, scream. Whatever it is that helps get you through the days, do it. You will experience the hurt, the denial, the anger, and, as time goes on, the acceptance and peace.

I believe that's the biggest task Mom set out to do before she passed away—to not only make peace herself with what was going to happen but to make sure those who loved her made peace with it as well. It became her sole mission. I can still hear her saying, "Accept the things you cannot change, the courage to change the things you can, and the wisdom to know the difference."

It is so difficult to prepare for losing a loved one. There wasn't anything I found right away that soothed my pain. But when it did, there was some comfort in knowing that

Mom was saved when she died. There was comfort in the memories. I know now that you still must keep God first and pray for strength when you are going through tough times such as losing a loved one.

There was comfort in knowing God's Word. We are to rejoice when people die and cry when they are born. I admit it was not my first thought at all. I cried, and I yelled … I did the exact opposite. Finding appropriate scriptures also helped. "And ye now therefore have sorrow: but I will see you again, and your heart shall rejoice, and your heart shall rejoice, and your joy no man taketh from you"(John 16:22). "Blessed are they that mourn: for they shall be comforted" (Matthew 5:4 KJV). And one scripture I think about for Mom is "I have fought a good fight, I have finished my course. I have kept the faith" (2 Timothy 4:7). That, my dear mom did for sure. I am encouraged to do the same by living my life as an example for a long as I live.

I know now when dealing with the probability of losing someone very close to you that you must become selfless for them. You must understand and know what it is your loved one wants, needs, and desires because it's all about that person. It's important to have the conversations if you don't know what it is your loved one needs and wants. Yes, it's hard but needed, as time is precious. You'll want to do everything you can to make your loved one happy. It helps make the transition for that person easier, and in the end, you'll be grateful that you did. The memories you'll have from those things you will be able to hold onto to help with your own comfort. No matter how small or large the task is, for those we love, we must do all we can to do it and make it happen. I am glad that we did and I didn't stay wrapped up in my own discontent.

Think of it this way: you may be upset that your loved one is at risk of losing his or her life but remember that your loved one is the one who is losing his or her life. That helped me put things into perspective. It was never all about me. It was all about Mom. If I could go back and deal with my emotions differently, that's one thing I would have done sooner. Take self out of the way immediately and *be there 100 percent, all the time.*

I remember Aunt Aggie telling me, "Don't you be mad, and don't question God. He makes no mistakes. It's all something we must go through one day. And you'll get to see your mom again. We all will. Let go of that anger. Your mom wouldn't want that. You know she loved you. You have great memories—more good than bad. Hold on to them. Hold on to them!" She was right, and it was the same thing my mom had told me. Confirmation.

I finally had come to terms with Mom's passing. She may have lost the battle to cancer, but she won the fight of this life!

CHAPTER 9

LETTING GO

As the years have passed, it still feels like yesterday that she left. Even writing this, the flood of tears came back just as if I were experiencing it eighteen years ago. Thank God that He sent the Comforter during my time of need! Losing Mom was a very emotional time for our family. I was so young at the time in my walk with the Lord and didn't fully understand how to handle death at all, especially losing someone so intimately close to me. I didn't know what to expect before or after. As I've matured over the years, I understand it now. I thank God for the thirty-seven years I had with Mom. I am thankful for all those special moments we shared in her lifetime, especially those in the final months. I'll cherish them forever. I'll always remember her voice, the beautiful alto sound of her voice singing, her laugh, her smile, and the feel of her warm embrace.

I did all I could to keep my focus after Mom had passed. I found myself picking up the phone to call her every day. I tried everything to keep busy. Many years afterward, I would still call to listen to the answering machine. Robert never changed the number or the message, as he knew I would call from time to time and listen to her voice. God bless him for that! I was desperate to hold onto anything of Mom's, so listening to her voice brought me comfort. I have a few of her belongings that I kept, and one was her trench coat. I found a handkerchief she left in the pocket that smells like the perfume she wore. I still pull it out to smell her scent on those days when I need something additional to help get me through.

Just as she had done on the birthday and anniversary of my brother's passing, I now light a candle on her birthday and the anniversary date when she passed. I still have those moments when something triggers a memory, and it stops me in my tracks. Now I can smile and look up, knowing she's finally resting and at peace. Mom will always be in my heart and with me. She will always be my favorite girl!

I was thirty-seven when Mom passed away. My family and other people who knew my mom often tell me I look like her. Especially when I go home to visit my aunties now, they always tell me, "You look just like Christine!"

That always makes me smile, but I don't have nearly half the beauty as the angel I affectionately remember as Mom. I strive to be like her, as she was the greatest influence in my life. My admiration of her being a God-fearing, selfless, forgiving woman lives on through me. When trials have come in my life, I often think about what Mom would do, and somehow it helps me to always make the right decision because what she would do is trust and keep God first.

The main lessons in life I learned from her were to live life to the fullest and not take it for granted because tomorrow isn't promised, forgive as our Father in heaven has forgiven us, trust God with all things keeping Him first, and love hard with a whole heart even when it's not easy. I try to live by these principles, as they have helped keep me grounded. As a way to honor my mom's memory over the years, I have participated in breast cancer awareness walks and whenever I hear of someone (whether I know them personally or not) going through chemotherapy, I donate Kindles.

Shortly after we laid Mom to rest, I had a dream that really comforted me. It scared me at first, as I wasn't sure what to think. In the dream, I walked into her bedroom, and she was sitting on her bed putting on her shoes. She looked up at me and smiled. She said, "I am getting ready to go."

This was surprising because she was so sick and not able to do anything or go anywhere on her own, let alone to be sitting up and talking to me like nothing was wrong. Mom then stood up fully dressed, still smiling at me. Before she left, she said, "I told you that I would be okay! They that wait on the Lord shall renew their strength."

I woke up looking around for her to see where she went. What had happened? It seemed so real—like she was right in the room with me.

I took the dream as confirmation she truly was okay. For the first time, I felt like everything was going to be okay because she let me know she was okay. It was closure that helped me come to terms with accepting she was gone. I felt like I could rejoice knowing she wasn't in pain and was no longer suffering. She had truly made it to the other side. It helped me accept she really had won. Until we see one another again, rest in peace, Mom. I will always remember and love you.

"But they that wait upon the Lord shall renew their strength; they shall mount up with wings as eagles; they shall run, and not be weary; and they shall walk, and not faint" (Isaiah 40:31 KJV).

Printed in the United States
By Bookmasters